THE REAL SPIRIT OF CHRISTMAS

A play for children

WES MAGEE

SAMUEL FRENCH

LONDON
NEW YORK TORONTO SYDNEY HOLLYWOOD

Copyright © 1978 by Samuel French Ltd
All Rights Reserved

THE REAL SPIRIT OF CHRISTMAS is fully protected under the copyright laws of the British Commonwealth, including Canada, the United States of America, and all other countries of the Copyright Union. All rights, including professional and amateur stage productions, recitation, lecturing, public reading, motion picture, radio broadcasting, television and the rights of translation into foreign languages are strictly reserved.

ISBN 978-0-573-06613-9

www.samuelfrench.co.uk
www.samuelfrench.com

For Amateur Production Enquiries

United Kingdom and World excluding north america

plays@SamuelFrench-London.co.uk

020 7255 4302/01

Each title is subject to availability from Samuel French,

depending upon country of performance.

CAUTION: Professional and amateur producers are hereby warned that THE REAL SPIRIT OF CHRISTMAS is subject to a licensing fee. Publication of this play does not imply availability for performance. Both amateurs and professionals considering a production are strongly advised to apply to the appropriate agent before starting rehearsals, advertising, or booking a theatre. A licensing fee must be paid whether the title is presented for charity or gain and whether or not admission is charged.

The professional rights in this play are controlled by Samuel French Ltd, 52 Fitzroy Street, London, W1T 5JR.

No one shall make any changes in this title for the purpose of production. No part of this book may be reproduced, stored in a retrieval system, or transmitted in any form, by any means, now known or yet to be invented, including mechanical, electronic, photocopying, recording, videotaping, or otherwise, without the prior written permission of the publisher. No one shall upload this title, or part of this title, to any social media websites.

The right of Wes Magee to be identified as author of this work has been asserted in accordance with Section 77 of the Copyright, Designs and Patents Act 1988.

CHARACTERS

Alfie Ruffcut
JoJo ⎫
Pip ⎬ his sisters
Dick ⎫
Sid ⎬ his brothers
Mother
Father
The Children at the Party (10 children)

North Pole Postman
North Pole Sorters (2 children)
North Pole letter-checker

Christmas Spirits (2 children)
Christmas Toy Factory People (7 children)
Foreman of the Factory
The Christmas Cracker Joke Writers (3 children)
Carol Singers (6 children)
Angels (8 to 10 children)
Father Christmas
His helpers (3 children)

The play offers a chance for 48 children to act, with every character (except the Angels) given dialogue to speak

The action of the play takes place in Alfie Ruffcut's house, and at various places visited by Alfie and the Spirits of Christmas

Time—the present

NOTES ON THE PLAY

The play is a fantasy/comedy but it has a serious message regarding Christmas and this should be underlined in a production. The play will get off to a vibrant start if the party scene is played with gusto and noise.

The star-ship can be simply made by cutting out a six-pointed star from a roll of corrugated paper. This can then be painted, named and fixed to a small display board. The giant cracker can be made in the same way from corrugated paper then covered with Christmas wrapping paper and "fronted" with a large silver star.

You may find that the musical items need to be recorded so that they can be played at the right times in the play.

Alfie Ruffcut will be effectively dressed if he wears black from head to toe to emphasize his black character. The Angels can carry stars on sticks and head-bands with stars attached to them. The Spirits can be dressed in white sheets and carry "thunder-and-lightning wands" (cardboard zig-zags attached to sticks)

W.M.

THE REAL SPIRIT OF CHRISTMAS

Scene 1

The living-room of the Ruffcuts' house

A Christmas party is under way. The Children are dancing to a modern Christmas record. After the first verse the children all join in with the chorus, and then the music fades

Jojo Just look at the dancing, it's great.
Pip It's fantastic.
Jojo The party's going with a bang.

Someone bursts a balloon

Pip Come on, Jojo, let's dance before the record finishes.

The dance continues. The Children again join in with the chorus. They finish the dance with a burst of applause

Child 1 That was smashing.
Child 2 Terrific party, Jojo.

Mother enters with a tray of mince pies

Jojo Wow, I'm boiling.
Pip Here comes Mother with the mince pies.
All Hurrah!
Mother Eat up, eat up everyone.
Jojo Yes, we've got another game coming soon.
Dick What about pass the parcel?
Sid What about pass the parcel?
Pip Oh, quiet, you two.
Jojo Listen everyone. Are you all enjoying the party?
All We sure are!
Mother Dick. Sid. Don't gobble those pies. You'll choke.
Dick Okay, Mum.
Sid Okay, Mum.
Pip Well, what about another game? What about pinning the tail on the donkey?

All Yes, ace, great!
Pip Come here, Anne, let me blindfold you.
Jojo Where's the donkey?
Child 3 Here, Jojo. (*She carries in a board with a donkey drawn on it*)
Child 4 Put it over here.
Child 5 Here's the donkey's tail.
Child 6 Spin Anne round, spin her round.

Pip and Jojo spin Anne round and round. She moves about the room trying to find the donkey on the board

All You're cold—colder—colder—getting warmer—getting warmer—almost hot—getting hot.

Alfie Ruffcut enters the room

Anne pins the tail—into Alfie Ruffcut

Alfie Ruffcut Ouch! You idiot!
Anne Have I found the donkey?
Jojo You certainly have, you've found the donkey all right. You've found my rotten brother Alfie Ruffcut.
Pip *Our* rotten brother Alfie Ruffcut.
All Oh, it's Alfie Ruffcut!
Sid } Awful old Alfie Ruffcut, our big brother. } (*Speaking together*)
Dick
Alfie Ruffcut What's going on here, then? What do you mean by pinning this donkey's tail on me, eh?
All Donkey! Donkey!
Alfie Ruffcut Clear off the lot of you. (*He kicks over the donkey board*)
All Stop That, Alfie Ruffcut!
Jojo It's our Christmas party.
Pip And you weren't invited.
Dick Yes, you weren't asked.
Sid Yes, you weren't asked.
Jojo No one asked you to come. Spoilsport!
Pip Party wrecker!
Dick Big twit!
Sid Big twit!
All Alfie Ruffcut: no-one asked *you* to the Christmas party.

Scene 1

Alfie Ruffcut Well I'm here now, so what are you going to do about it, eh? Ah, all gone quiet now, haven't you. Thought that you'd have a party without telling me, did you?
Jojo And we're going to finish our party, so there.
Dick So there.
Sid So there.
Alfie Ruffcut Oh no, you're not. I'll just burst these balloons for a start. (*He bursts three balloons*) Now who wants to carry on with the party, eh? You're all nuts, the lot of you. Christmas, huh, I don't believe a word about it.
All Stop that, Alfie Ruffcut.
Child 1 Don't believe in Christmas?
Alfie Ruffcut Not a word of it. It's all a load of kippers. Next you'll be telling there's such a person—(*he sniggers*)—as Father Christmas.
Jojo There is.
Pip Yes, there is.
Alfie Ruffcut Nonsense. He's nothing but an old man dressed up in the supermarket. Go on, the lot of you.
Jojo Don't cry, Anne. He's the horriblest—
Pip —nastiest—
Dick —terriblest—
Sid —terriblest—
All —boy in the world. That's Alfie Ruffcut! He's nobody's friend!
Alfie Ruffcut Clear off, the lot of you, clear off! (*He raises his fists*)

The Children exit, squealing and crying

Alfie wanders about the room, kicking balloons and streamers. He comes to the front of the stage

I'll teach that lot of kids to call *me* donkey. I'm not a donkey, am I? Donkey's are daft, we all know that. I'm not daft, am I? But honestly, what a bunch of stupid brothers and sisters I've got. I mean, there's Jojo. She's as nutty as a bag of peanuts. Just look at her.

Jojo enters and walks across the room; she ignores Alfie

And then there's Pip. Orange Pip, I call her. Just look at her.

Pip enters and walks across the room, picking up streamers

She's enough to give anyone the pip! And then there's those two kid brothers of mine, Dick and Sid. Hey, here they come now.

Dick and Sid enter

Dick You've messed up our party, Alfie.
Sid You've messed up our party, Alfie.
Alfie Ruffcut So what, kids?
Dick Our friends have all gone home.
Sid Our friends have all gone home.
Alfie Ruffcut They should call you two Polly and Wolly. You're like a pair of parrots repeating everything like that.
Dick Take no notice of him.
Sid Take no notice of him.
Dick He's a nasty piece of work.
Sid He's a nasty piece of work.
Dick At least we can do cartwheels, which he can't.
Sid At least we can do cartwheels, which he can't.

Dick and Sid do a series of cartwheels, to drum rolls, then exit

Alfie Ruffcut What a pair of parrots. Well, that's that. I've wrecked their stupid party. Christmas, indeed. It's all a load of kippers. But I've still managed to get my sisters and brothers some presents, some really *nasty* presents. Look, I've got a giant polo for Jojo. And an old brown apple core for Pip. There's plenty of pips in it, heh, heh. And a box of parrot food for Dick and Sid. Oh yes, I'm going to have a rare old time wrecking their Christmas this year, I'll give them a Christmas to remember.

Alfie exits

Scene 2

The Children are writing their letters to Father Christmas. Mother and Father are sitting watching them

Mother How did your party go, Jojo?
Jojo Not very well.
Father Why not, Jojo?
Jojo Alfie Ruffcut ruined it.
Mother Alfie? What was he doing there?

Scene 2

Pip He wasn't invited.
Jojo Yet he came and ruined our party.
Dick He's a nasty big-head.
Sid He's a nasty big-head.
Mother Well, never mind about him now. It's Christmas Eve, and we should think good things about everyone—even Alfie Ruffcut.
Father Even so he's growing up into a most peculiar boy. What are you all doing?
Dick We're writing—
Sid —our letters—
Dick ⎫
Sid ⎭ To Father Christmas. (*Speaking together*)
Jojo We're asking him for presents—stacks of them.
Pip I've nearly finished mine.
Mother What have you asked for?
Jojo A doll that hiccups—
Pip —and a pair of roller-skates—
Dick —and I want a scooter.
Sid And I want a scooter.
Father And you think that you'll get them all?
Jojo I *know* we will.
Mother Well, I think that you should ask for a *present for Alfie*.
Jojo ⎱ For Alfie? You're joking! He wrecked our ⎰ (*Speaking*
Pip ⎰ Christmas party! ⎱ *together*)
Mother But he *is* your brother, so why not show the real spirit of Christmas and ask Father Christmas to bring him a surprise.
Jojo Well, I'll ask that he believes in Father Christmas.
Pip And I'll ask for him to have the real Christmas spirit instead of all the anger he has now. The—real—Christmas—spirit.

The Children, Mother, and Father exit as the Lights dim

Scene 3

The Post Office at the North Pole

A gale is blowing as the Sorters set up their desk. The Letter-checker stands behind them. They sort letters until the North Pole Postman arrives with his sack full of letters

Postman Here you are, another sack load of letters for Father Christmas. (*He empties the letters on to the desk*)

Sorter 1 It's a real rush now. How many letters have we received?

Checker Nearly twenty thousand, and still one hour to go before midnight on Christmas Eve.

Postman Any interesting letters in that lot?

Sorter 1 Yes, one here from Peter Pan. "Dear Santa," it says, "don't forget to send me a new sword. I have that villain Captain Hook to eal with. It's time he was hooked and cooked for ever."

The Postman exits

Checker Still more letters coming in.

The Postman returns with yet another sack. He empties the letters on to the desk

Sorter 2 Hey, what about this letter.

Postman Who's it from?

Sorter 2 Someone called—Pip.

Sorter 1 What does she ask for?

Sorter 2 She asks for a pair of roller-skates—and, wait a minute, she says that her big brother Alfie Ruffcut doesn't believe in Father Christmas, and can he please be given the real spirit of Christmas.

Postman He sounds like a good person . .

Sorter 1 For the Christmas journey.

Checker Not *the* Christmas journey!

All Yes, the Christmas journey.

Sorter 2 This is *just* the letter we have been waiting for.

Sorter 1 We'd better tell the Christmas spirits.

Postman Oh dear, poor old Alfie Ruffcut, he doesn't know what is going to hit him in the middle of the night this Christmas Eve.

Sorters He'll know soon enough, he'll know!

The Sorters exit

Postman Look out, Alfie Ruffcut. Look out when you're fast asleep tonight. The Christmas Spirits—are—coming—for—you!

The Postman and the Checker exit as the Lights dim

Scene 4

Alfie Ruffcut's bedroom. Christmas Eve

Alfie enters in his pyjamas. He listens as the clock strikes midnight

Alfie Ruffcut Christmas, huh, it's all a load of kippers. (*He listens*) Not a sound. All the family dreaming their heads off. Well, time for bed. (*He looks out of the window*) Hum, just starting to snow, and not a sign of Father Christmas, as if there ever could be. Like I told Jojo and Pip and Dick and Sid—it's all a load of kippers. Ho hum—now where's that horror comic? (*He climbs into bed*) Ah, the green beast from the pit of acid—lovely stuff—yes—time—for—sleep...

After a few seconds the light increases and space music is heard

> *Two figures dressed in white float and dance across the stage. They move around Alfie's bed, then suddenly tap him on the back with their lightning-and-thunder sticks.*

Alfie Ruffcut Whatsmarrer—what's up? YIKES! GHOSTS!
Spirit 1 We're not ghosts.
Spirit 2 We're the Spirits of Christmas.
Alfie Ruffcut GHOSTS! HELP ME, MOTHER! GHOSTS!
Spirit 1 I'm the Spirit of Christmas Kindness.
Spirit 2 And I'm the Spirit of Christmas Happiness.
Spirits And we've come to take *you* on the Christmas journey.
Alfie Ruffcut The Christmas journey?
Spirit Right first time.
Spirit 2 Come on, come on, Father Christmas mustn't be kept waiting.
Alfie Ruffcut F...F...Father Christmas! Father Christmas!
Spirit 1 Yes, we know all about you, Alfie Ruffcut.
Spirit 2 And we're going to prove to you that Father Christmas really does exist.
Spirit 1 So come on, time you were going on the Christmas journey.
Alfie Ruffcut Oh Yikes! But I can't fly.
Spirit 2 No trouble. You're travelling by the S—T—A—R.
Alfie Ruffcut S—T—A—R? Now that rings a bell.

Spirit 1 And so it should. What have the children been shouting at you this Christmas?
Alfie Ruffcut They've shouted: "Stop That, Alfie Ruffcut."
Spirit 2 S for Stop, T for That, A for Alfie, and R for Ruffcut.
Spirit 1 S—T—A—R. And that's what you're travelling in to the land of Christmas dreams.

A large star-ship appears on the stage

Alfie Ruffcut Oh, Mother, help me!
Spirit 2 Too late, boy.
Spirit 1 Step aboard the star-ship. Here we go.

Space music. The two Spirits and Alfie Ruffcut go "inside" the star-ship that has appeared on stage. Lights flash

Scene 5

The Christmas Toy Factory

The space music stops, and the two Spirits and Alfie Ruffcut emerge from behind the star-ship

Spirit 1 Here we are. The first stop on your Christmas journey.
Spirit 2 The Christmas Toy Factory.
Spirit 1 Shhhhh. Here comes the Foreman of the factory.

The two Spirits and Alfie Ruffcut stand aside

The Foreman enters. He carries a placard which says "I'M IN CHARGE"

Foreman Now then. Where's the toy machine? Come on, come on, you lot, old Father Christmas has ordered us to make some more toys for his sack.

Seven Children walk stiffly on to the stage. They are dressed similarly and each child carries a large letter on his/her chest: M, A, C, H, I, N, E. Their faces are "frozen" and they stand like statues waiting for the Foreman to start the "machine"

Right then, everything ready? (*He inspects the "machine"*) Just pull the lever, and Bob's your uncle, and Fanny's your aunt.

Scene 5

The "machine" goes into action. One after the other the seven Children perform different machine movements, plus noises. The Foreman nips along to the end of the "machine" where he lifts out a toy. He does this twice, dropping the toys into a large sack

Right then, that's the lot. This lot will fill up a few Christmas stockings. Time to be going, I reckon. Old Father Christmas will be itching to get away in his sleigh.

The Foreman exits, and the "machine" Children follow him, walking stiffly

Spirit 1 Well there you are, Alfie Ruffcut.
Spirit 2 The Christmas Toy Factory.
Spirit 1 Time to move on again.
Alfie Ruffcut Move on? Where are we going now?
Spirits Just wait and see, wait and see.

They go back "inside" the star-ship. Space music, and the Lights flash

Scene 6

The Christmas Cracker Joke Workshop

The two Spirits and Alfie emerge once more from the star-ship

Spirit 1 Part two of the Christmas journey.
Spirit 2 The Christmas Cracker Joke Workshop
Alfie Ruffcut YIKES!
Spirit 1 This is where all the jokes for Christmas crackers are written.
Alfie Ruffcut You're joking!
Spirit 1 I'm not—but *they* are!

The two Spirits and Alfie stand aside

Joke Writer 1 enters

Joker 1 Now where's that giant Christmas cracker that we have to fill?

Joke Writers 2 and 3 enter with the giant cracker

Joker 2
Joker 3 } Here it is, boss. (*Speaking together*)

Joker 1 Well, put it down here.

Joker 2 Who's it for, this giant cracker?

Joker 1 It's for the BBC television. Seems like they need a heap of jokes for their comedians.

Joker 2 I think we've just about run out of new jokes.

Joker 3 Well, let's try and think of a few, then we can get back to bed and sleep until next Christmas.

They walk up and down the stage deep in thought

Joker 2 I've got one. (*They hold up their "joke" cards*) What's yellow, and swings from tree to tree?

Joker 1
Joker 3 } No idea. (*Speaking together*).

Joker 2 Tarzipan! BOOM! BOOM!

Joker 1 That'll do. Put it in the cracker. Who's got another joke?

Joker 3 I have. What goes Ha! Ha! BONK?

They hold up their "joke" cards

Joker 1
Joker 2 } No idea. (*Speaking together*)

Joker 3 A man laughing his head off! BOOM! BOOM!

Joker 1 What about a "knock knock" joke?

Joker 2
Joker 3 } Okay. (*Speaking together*)

They hold up their "joke" cards

Joker 1 Knock, Knock.

Joker 2
Joker 3 } Who's there? (*Speaking together*)

Joker 1 Mary.

Joker 2
Joker 3 } Mary who? (*Speaking together*)

Joker 1 Mary Christmas! BOOM! BOOM!

Joker 2 Put it in the cracker. I think that's enough.

Joker 3 Just one more for good luck.

Joker 1 Why do bees hum?

They hold up their "joke" cards

Scene 6

Joker 2 ⎫
Joker 3 ⎬ No idea. (*Speaking together*)

Joker 1 Because they don't know the words. 'Bye, 'bye.

Joker 1 runs off, pursued by Joker 2 and Joker 3, who carry off the giant cracker

There is a good deal of noise and shouting

Spirit 1 Come on, Alfie Ruffcut, no time to waste.
Spirit 2 Yes, we must get on to the next stop on your Christmas journey.
Alfie Ruffcut Where to now, where?
Spirits Wait and see, wait and see.

They go back "inside" the star-ship. Space music, and Lights flash.

Scene 7

Outside Alfie Ruffcut's house

The star-ship arrives outside the house. The two Spirits and Alfie emerge once more

Spirit 1 Here we are, stop number three.
Spirit 2 Do you know where you are?
Alfie Ruffcut Wait a minute—I'm outside *my* house, *my own* house.
Spirit 1 Right. And listen.
Spirit 2 Yes, listen. Can you hear singing?

They stand aside

The six Carol Singers enter, carrying lanterns, and dressed in coats, bobble-hats, and boots. They walk around the stage singing the first verse and chorus of "The First Nowell". They come to a stop outside the Ruffcuts' front door

Carol Singers Christmas is coming, the geese are getting fat.
　　　　　　　Please put a penny in the old man's hat.
　　　　　　　If you haven't got a penny a half will do,
　　　　　　　If you haven't got a half, then God Bless You!

Jojo and Pip emerge from the Ruffcuts' front door and drop coins into the collecting-boxes

Pip \
Jojo } MERRY CHRISTMAS! (*Speaking together*) \
Carol Singers MERRY CHRISTMAS, and A HAPPY NEW YEAR!

Jojo and Pip return through the front door. The Carol Singers exit singing the first verse and chorus of "The First Nowell")

Spirit 1 Did you see your sisters giving money to the carol singers?
Spirit 2 They've got the *real* spirit of Christmas.
Alfie Ruffcuff But—but my sisters are in bed and asleep. How can they be up and dressed in the middle of night—on Christams Eve?
Spirit 1 Remember, you are on the Christmas journey.
Spirit 2 Time means nothing now. We can take you to the past or to the future.
Spirit 1 We can take you anywhere.
Alfie Ruffcut Anywhere?
Spirit 2 To the dawn of time itself. When the world was wobbly as a jelly.
Spirit 1 Or to the ends of the universe.
Spirit 2 Or under the green ice at the North Pole.
Spirit 1 Or to the ends of the rainbow.
Spirit 2 But now you're going to the skies above Bethlehem.
Spirit 1 Where the angels are gathering to watch over baby Jesus as he lies in the manger.

The two Spirits and Alfie go "inside" the star-ship. Space sounds, and Lights flash

Scene 8

The skies above Bethlehem

An instrumental recording of "Silent Night" heralds the entrance of the Angels. They come on stage, one at a time, and move slowly to the music until all eight or ten finally form a tableau. The final

Scene 8

tableau will coincide with the end of the recorded music. This gives great effect if, finally, the angels gather at the front of the stage, some kneeling, some standing, with arms upraised as if they are watching over the manger. *The Lights go down to Black-out*

SCENE 9

The North Pole

Space Sounds and Lights flash. The Spirits and Alfie emerge from the star-ship for the last time

Spirit 1 Here we are. The last visit on your Christmas journey.
Alfie Ruffcut It's blooming cold. Where are we?
Spirit 2 The North Pole.
Spirit 1 The land of ice and snow.
Spirit 2 You've come to meet Father Christmas.
Spirit 1 Before he sets off on his sleigh.
Alfie Ruffcut F ... F ... Father Christmas! You mean, he really is *real*?
Spirits Wait and see, wait and see.

They stand aside

"Jingle Bells" music is heard, and Father Christmas enters with a sack slung over his shoulder. He hops around to the music, trying to warm his frozen toes. His three Helpers also come on stage

Father Christmas Well, are we all set?
Helpers All set, Father Christmas.
Father Christmas Bit chilly, isn't it?
Helpers Sure is, old white whiskers.
Father Christmas What's the time? Are we early or late?
Helpers Right on time, Mr Red Nose.
Father Christmas Are all the toys packed in my sack?
Helpers All packed Mr Big Black Boots.
Father Christmas And the reindeer, are they harnessed to my sleigh?
Helpers All ready and waiting for your word, Santa Claus.
Father Christmas Who snores?

Helpers Claus, not snores, Santa!
Father Christmas Wait a bit, hang about, hold on, now just look'ee here. Who's this out of his warm beddy weddy on a freezing Christmas Eve like this?
Spirit 1 (*stepping forward*) I am the Spirit of Christmas Kindness.
Spirit 2 (*stepping forward*) And I am the Spirit of Christmas Happiness.
Helpers Wow! We thought you were a couple of ghosts!
Father Christmas Take no notice of that hignorant bunch of helpers.
Helpers Huh! Mr Bossy Bags!
Father Christmas But who's this in his pyjamas?
Spirit 1 Alfie Ruffcut.
Spirit 2 He's on the Christmas journey.
Father Christmas You mean, that he's—
Spirits —the one person who doesn't believe in YOU!
Father Christmas Doesn't believe in me, eh?
Alfie Ruffcut Well . . .
Father Christmas Well, come here, lad.

Alfie slowy approaches

Is this real? (*He indicates his beard*)

Alfie touches the beard

Are these real? (*He holds out his arms*)

Alfie pats the arms

Am I *real*?

Alfie walks around Father Christmas

Alfie Ruffcut Yes—yes you are real. You *are* real!
Helpers Of course he's real, aren't you, Santa Claus.
Father Christmas Who snores?
Helpers Oh Claus, not snores, Santa!
Father Christmas Well, nice to meet you, Alfie Ruffcut. But no more time to waste in gassing. I've got to get these presents delivered. Ready to fly?
Helpers Ready to go, Old White Whiskers.
Father Christmas On your way then. 'Bye, 'bye, all.
Helpers 'Bye, 'bye, all. Come on Mr Big Black Boots, come on.

Scene 9

Father Christmas and the Helpers exit to the sound of "Jingle Bells"

Spirit 1 Time you were going home, Alfie.
Spirit 2 Time you were back in bed.
Alfie Ruffcut I'll say! I'm near frozen out here at the North Pole.

The Spirits and Alfie go "inside" the star-ship. Space sounsd, and Lights flash

Scene 10

The Ruffcuts' living-room. Christmas Day morning

A clock strikes eight. Jojo enters with Pip: Jojo has a doll, Pip a pair of roller-skates

Jojo Look, I got my doll that hiccups.
Pip And I got my roller-skates.

Dick and Sid enter with their scooters

Dick Look, I got my scooter.
Sid Look, I got my scooter.

They ride them around the stage

All I wonder what rotten old Alfie Ruffcut got for Christmas?

Alfie Ruffcut enters and goes over to Dick's scooter

Alfie Ruffcut Hello, kids.
All Stop That, Alfie Ruffcut!
Alfie Ruffcut No, don't say that, please.
Jojo Eh? What's the matter with him?
Pip Has he gone soft in his head?
Alfie Ruffcut I've—I've changed my mind about Christmas, that's all.
All What?
Alfie Ruffcut I just believe in Father Christmas, that's all.
All Alfie Ruffcut, believes in Father Christmas? You're joking!
Alfie Ruffcut You don't know a thing, you lot. I've been places.
Jojo What places?

Alfie Ruffcut I've been on the Christmas journey.
Pip Christmas journey?
Dick What are you talking about?
Sid What are you talking about?
Alfie Ruffcut I've been to places, like the North Pole, and the Christmas Cracker Joke Workshop, and the skies above Bethlehem. I've even met Father Christmas. I touched him.
All Prove it, Alfie Ruffcut, prove it.
Alfie Ruffcut Well—well I can't . . . (*He wanders about the stage, then suddenly feels in the top pocket of his pyjamas. He pulls out a tiny star*) What's this?
Jojo It's a star.
Pip Is it real?
Alfie Ruffcut Course it's real. It must be from the spirits.
Jojo What spirits?
Alfie Ruffcut The Spirits of Christmas. Oh come on, let's go to breakfast and I'll tell you all about it. And remember, no more of that "Stop That, Alfie Ruffcut". What you were really saying was S—T—A—R. And that's what I've got now, a star. It will help me to remember the Christmas journey, and that Christmas *really* is a time for kindness and happiness. Come on, kids, let's have breakfast.

They all exit, Alfie putting his arms round their shoulders as they go

The Lights dim to a Black-out. The cast assemble on the stage during the first verse of the Christmas song played at the beginning. The Lights come up and everyone finally joins in the chorus, so repeating the party atmosphere that existed at the start of the play, as—

the CURTAIN *falls*

FURNITURE AND PROPERTY LIST

Note: On-stage furniture for Scene 1 is stacked against the sides to allow for dancing. Furniture and props for succeeding scenes are set and struck by the cast

On stage: 2 small armchairs
3 children's desks with stools. *In them:* pens, notepaper
Table. *On it:* various dishes of "party" foods
On floor, walls, etc.: balloons, streamers

Off stage: Tray of mince pies **(Mother)**
Board with donkey drawn on it, tail with pin **(Child 3)**
Post Office Sorters' desk with letters **(Cast, for Scene 3)**
2 sacks of letters **(Postman)**
Small bed and bedding **(Cast, for Scene 4)**
Window flat **(Cast, for Scene 4)**
Star-ship (see Production Note)
I'M IN CHARGE placard **(Foreman)**
M-A-C-H-I-N-E letters **(Children)**
2 toys **(Children)**
Giant cracker **(Jokers)**
Joke cards **(Jokers)**
Front door flat **(Cast, for Scene 7)**
Lanterns, collecting-boxes **(Carol Singers)**
Coins **(Jojo, Pip)**
Stars **(Angels)**
Sack of toys **(Father Christmas)**
Doll **(Jojo)**
Roller-skates **(Pip)**
Scooters **(Dick, Sid)**
Small star **(Alfie)**

LIGHTING PLOT

Property fittings required: nil
Open stage

To open: General lighting full up

| Cue 1 | **Alfie:** "... a Christmas to remember." (*He exits*) (Page 4)
Fade to Black-out: return to previous lighting when Scene 2 set

| Cue 2 | **Pip:** "The—real—Christmas—spirit." (Page 5)
Fade to Black-out: bring up cold, wintry lighting on Post Office when ready

| Cue 3 | **Postman:** "... are—coming—for—you!" (Page 6)
Fade to Black-out: bring up spot on Alfie's bed when ready

| Cue 4 | **Alfie:** "... time—for—sleep." (Page 7)
Pause, bring up dim general lighting

| Cue 5 | **Spirits:** "Here we go." (Page 8)
Flashing lights—continue through scene change to general lighting

| Cue 6 | **Spirits:** "... wait and see.' (Page 9)
Flashing lights—continue through scene change to general lighting

| Cue 7 | **Spirits:** "... wait and see." (Page 11)
Flashing lights—continue through scene change to spot on front door

| Cue 8 | **Spirit 1:** "... in the manger." (Page 12)
Flashing lights—continue through scene change to golden glow on Angels

| Cue 9 | As "Silent Night" music ends (Page 13)
Fade to Black-out: follow with flashing lights through scene change to cold frosty North Pole lighting

| Cue 10 | **Alfie:** "... at the North Pole." (Page 15)
Flashing lights—continue through scene change to bright general overall lighting

| Cue 11 | **Children** exit (Page 16)
Fade to Black-out: bring up all lighting to full when cast assembled

EFFECTS PLOT

Cue 1	**To open** *Music: continue until dance finishes*	(Page 1)
Cue 2	**Dick** and **Sid** exit doing cartwheels *Drum roll*	(Page 4)
Cue 3	**During Scene 3** *Howling wind effect*	(Page 5)
Cue 4	**At start of Scene 4** *Clock strikes midnight*	(Page 7)
Cue 5	**As Spirits enter** *Space music*	(Page 7)
Cue 6	**Spirits and Alfie enter star-ship** *Space music until they emerge*	(Page 8)
Cue 7	**Spirits and Alfie enter star-ship** *Space music until they emerge*	(Page 9)
Cue 8	**Spirits and Alfie enter star-ship** *Space music until they emerge*	(Page 11)
Cue 9	**Spirits and Alfie enter star-ship** *Space music until they emerge*	(Page 12)
Cue 10	**During Scene 8** *Music: "Silent Night"*	(Page 12)
Cue 11	**As Lights fade to Black-out** *Space music until Spirits and Alfie emerge*	(Page 13)
Cue 12	**As Father Christmas enters** *Music: "Jingle Bells"—repeat as he exits*	(Page 13)
Cue 13	**Spirits and Alfie enter star-ship** *Space music: continue until start of Scene 10*	(Page 15)
Cue 14	**As Scene 10 opens** *Clock strikes eight*	(Page 15)
Cue 15	**As Lights come up for finale** *Music*	(Page 16)

www.ingramcontent.com/pod-product-compliance
Lightning Source LLC
Chambersburg PA
CBHW070456050426
42450CB00012B/3302